D0975327

Why Do Birds Sing?

A **Just Ask**™ Book

by Chris Arvetis
and Carole Palmer

illustrated by
Vernon McKissack

FIELD PUBLICATIONS
MIDDLETOWN, CT.

You did —
and it's a bird!
Lots of birds sing.

She knows everything !

Well, I am a bird.
When I sing, you hear
"Hoot, hoot!"
There are many kinds
of song birds.
Each kind has its
own song.

Hoot!

They do?

I hear you!

From morning to night, birds can be heard singing.

A bird talks to other birds with its song.

In early spring, the male bird sings to find a mate.

Once a mate is found, the bird sings more songs as it builds a nest.

Then the bird uses warning calls to keep other birds away from the nesting place.

When the baby birds are born, they use calls to get attention.
The peeping and chirping noises let mother bird know they are hungry or frightened.

They never stop!

Some sparrows and whippoorwills sing best at night.
The house wren sings a happy song all day long.

Some birds have calls
that say their name.

The Blue Jay says,
"Jay, Jay!"

The Chickadee chirps,
"Chick-A-Dee-Dee!"

The Bobwhite calls,
"Bob-White!"

The Cuckoo says,
"Cuckoo, Cuckoo!"

Bob-White!

The Mockingbird is very talented.
It can sound like any bird.
It can also cry like a cat or croak like a frog.
It mocks or *imitates* any sound it has heard.

Unbelievable!

Birds sing warning calls. The sharp "Caw" of the Crow lets other birds know of danger.

Birds call to each other when they want to get together.

These songs are called gathering calls.

You can hear gathering calls in the fall when birds get ready to fly south.

The honking geese and quacking ducks make loud gathering calls.

Quack!

Baby birds chirp for attention.
Loud calls give warnings.
Birds give calls to get together.
The birds sing to find mates
and build nests.
The bird songs fill the air
with music!

I love those sounds!